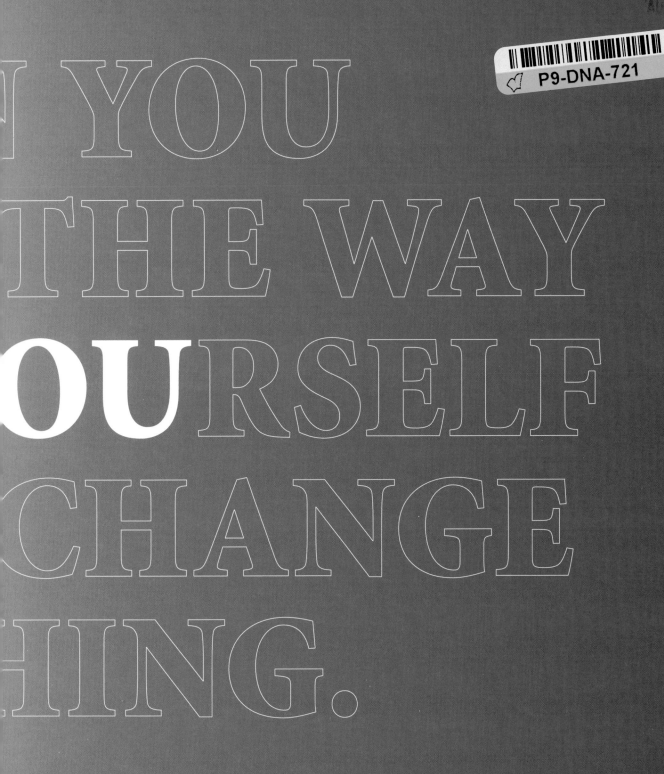

YOU

THE WAY

OURSELF

CHANGE

HING.

AUG 1 2006

P9-DNA-721

© 2008 by The Cramer Institute and The Concept Farm
All rights reserved under the Pan-American and
International Copyright Conventions

This book may not be reproduced in whole or in part,
in any form or by any means, electronic or mechanical,
including photocopying, recording, or by any information
storage and retrieval system now known or hereafter
invented, without written permission from the publisher.

Asset-based® Thinking

Asset-Based Thinking is the copyrighted property of:

The Concept Farm

9 8 7 6 5 4 3 2 1
Digit on the right indicates the number of this printing
Library of Congress Control Number: 2007940490
ISBN: 978-0-7624-3284-4

Printed in China

Running Press Book Publishers
2300 Chestnut Street
Philadelphia, Pennsylvania 19103

Visit us on the web:
www.runningpress.com
www.assetbasedthinking.com

This book may be ordered by mail from the publisher.
Please include $2.50 for postage and handling. But
try your bookstore first!

CHANGE
THE WAY YOU
SEE
YOURSELF

THROUGH ASSET-BASED THINKING®

DISCARDED
BRADFORD WG
PUBLIC LIBRARY

KATHRYN D. CRAMER, PH.D. + HANK WASIAK

RUNNING PRESS
PHILADELPHIA • LONDON

BRADFORD WG LIBRARY
100 HOLLAND COURT, BOX 130
BRADFORD, ONT. L3Z 2A7

TABLE OF CONTENTS

ABT

ACTION

POWER

INFLUENCE

IMPACT

ONWARD

THE ADVENTURE OF A LIFETIME.

To Change the Way You See Yourself through Asset-Based Thinking (ABT) is both a simple and profound experience. It takes courage and a sense of adventure.

ABT favors inspiration and aspiration over desperation. It propels your momentum, and dramatically increases your chances of being successful. It's infectious.

Let Asset-Based Thinking show you how to unleash your power, your influence, and your impact. That is what this book is all about.

THE ABT MIND-SET –
DON'T LEAVE HOME WITHOUT IT!

What ABT is:

Asset-Based Thinking is a way of viewing reality. Asset-Based Thinkers embrace the positive side of life and free themselves of the deficit-based negative side (DBT). ABT reveals how even the slightest shifts in your thinking can lead to seismic differences. This new mind-set was brought to life in the first bestseller of this series, *Change the Way You See Everything*.

How ABT works:

ABT is looking at yourself and the world through the eyes of what's working and your present strengths and potentials. With ABT you block out distractions and create a focal point of concentration and high mental energy centered on assets. ABT keeps you alert and inspired until you have maximized all there is to gain.

DBT FOCUS

- What you don't want
- What you need
- What is problematic
- What you can't do
- What isn't working
- Who is against you
- What is holding you back
- What you stand to lose
- Your setbacks

ABT FOCUS

- What you want

- What you have

- What is possible

- What you can do

- What is working

- Who is with you

- What is propelling you forward

- What you stand to gain

- Your achievements

ASSET-BASED THINKER'S S.O.S.

S.O.S. is recognized as the universal signal for help. But in ABT terms it is an acronym that helps you focus on where to look for assets.

Self "S"
Reminds you to look within yourself for your talents and strengths that are most useful in any circumstance.

Others "O"
Refers to your focus on the strengths and talents of others, and the positive qualities in your relationships (such as trust, respect, collaboration).

Situations "S"
Stands for the assets inherent in any situation. Good experiences naturally provide assets such as stimulation, opportunity, and synergy. But even unwelcome situations contain important assets such as vital new perspectives and life lessons.

Adventure is not out-
side man; it is within.

DAVID GRAYSON

This is the true joy in life, the being used for a purpose you consider a mighty one, the being a force of nature, rather than a feverish, selfish clod of ailments and grievances complaining that the world will not devote itself to making you happy.

GEORGE BERNHARD SHAW

CALL YOURSELF
TO ACTION

FROM REACTIVE TO PROACTIVE

Calling yourself to action means being proactive. In the face of the relentless barrage of daily demands, being proactive is not that easy. In fact, if you are like most people you operate in a reactive mode – consumed by deadlines at work, family obligations, household chores, and unexpected mishaps. You wake up feeling overwhelmed by what is urgent. You are busier than ever, but just barely able to keep up. Days, months, years fly by and you are left wondering, "where did the time go?", "what have I accomplished?", "whose tune am I marching to?"

With Asset-Based Thinking, life doesn't have to be a 24-7 treadmill. When you change the way you see yourself, you treat your personal priorities with the same level of importance as you do external demands. You set your sights on what you have to contribute, on what you want to make happen, on how you want to lead and inspire others.

Asset-Based Thinking helps you navigate through the ups and downs by letting your purpose and passions guide the way. Your life becomes an adventure of your own making. You put yourself in the driver's seat. You decide the destinations. You use surprise, serendipity, and even setbacks to make the journey more interesting and more worthwhile. You are more confident in who you are, where you are going, and how to get there. That is what **Change the Way You See Yourself** is all about.

UNLEASH YOUR POWER: IT'S THE FOUNDATION

The first step to being proactive, and putting yourself in the driver's seat, is to tap into your deepest reservoirs of personal power. Personal power comes from leveraging the assets that make you, "you." Like everyone, you have a unique combination of talents that inspire others and make you effective under almost any circumstance. One secret to unleashing personal power is to know which of your strengths and capabilities have made lasting, positive impressions and impacts.

In ABT terms, the unique set of assets that makes you stand out is your **Signature Presence**. When you step into your Signature Presence, you are the most authentic, compelling person you can be. You embody your beliefs. You allow your passion to shine through everything you say and do. **Your Signature Presence powers your ability to lead others** and to get exponentially better results. No matter what challenges come your way, your Signature Presence power will ensure you meet them.

EXPAND YOUR INFLUENCE: YOU CAN'T GET THERE ALONE

Putting yourself in the driver's seat doesn't mean you'll be traveling alone. Because you know where you are going, others with similar visions will want to join you. There will be people in your front seat, people riding in the backseat, and a whole caravan following close behind. People you have known for years, and some you have just met, will get on board.

As an Asset-Based Thinker, your job is to know your traveling companions as well as you know yourself. What makes each person tick? What does each one dream about? Most deeply desire? What kind of assets does each person bring to the adventure? Answering these questions helps you establish deep, rewarding relationships that form robust **circles of influence.**

Often you will ask, "who else wants to drive for a while?", "what side trips do you want to take?" As you invite others to navigate with you, the adventure becomes more exciting, more motivating, more energizing for everyone involved. **All of a sudden it's not just my adventure, it's our adventure.** You have attracted others to your cause. You have expanded the breadth and depth of your influence. With ABT you take your ability to be influential to a whole new level.

MAXIMIZE YOUR IMPACT:
DISCOVER YOUR INTERNAL PRIORITIES FIRST

Instead of being preoccupied with scanning the external world for what needs mastering or fixing, take a good, long look inside … see beyond your roles, responsibilities, and obligations. Focus on the visions of what you want to make happen.

Reflect on:
• Your deepest desires and longings
• Your sense of purpose
• Your passions
• Your "what ifs"
• Your dreams

Zoom in on the kind of impact you – the unique, talented you – want to make. Think of these aims as your **Signature Impacts**. The impacts that have your name on them and call you to action.

The visions that mean the most to you give you insight into your mighty cause. In ABT terms, **your mighty cause is the one you were born to serve**. This is your deepest source of inspiration, and the one that gives you the best chance of maximizing your impact.

Connect the dots:

List, Connect, & Discover

Inventory your personal priorities. Use this chart to get started. Connect your personal priorities to wider-world agendas. Discover how you can energize your personal world to have greater impact in the wider world.

Be Aware

The contributions you make in your personal world are the essential building blocks of your contributions to the wider world. Being more aware of the strides you make daily helps you see new ways of advancing wider world agendas.

Open Doors

Just by being the "true you," the distance between you and your goals will get shorter. Doors will start opening in unexpected ways. You will see clearly how you can make your impact matter.

Create Bridges

PERSONAL PRIORITIES	WIDER-WORLD AGENDAS
Working hard to provide for your family	Raising the standard of living for all people and nations
Exercising, eating well, living a balanced, healthy lifestyle	Curing AIDS and cancer
Seeking to understand and respect people with different opinions and backgrounds	Eliminating genocide and ethnic cleansing
Conserving energy/water	Renewing the world's energy and water supplies
Recycling	Reversing global warming
Raising children and grandchildren	Protecting, nurturing, and educating every child
Talking things out to resolve conflict	Advancing world peace
Living up to your commitments	Building world alliances
YOUR PERSONAL ACTIONS	WIDER-WORLD AGENDAS
YOUR PERSONAL ACTIONS	WIDER-WORLD AGENDAS
YOUR PERSONAL ACTIONS	WIDER-WORLD AGENDAS

Go for it

YOUR MIGHTY CAUSE: IT'S YOUR REASON FOR BEING

To lead a significant life, you have to dedicate yourself to a mighty cause – the one you feel born to serve. Calling yourself to action in service of a worthy cause gives meaning to your life. Once you commit yourself you get an automatic boost. Being alive doesn't get any better than this.

So, why do so many of us:

• Sell ourselves short?
• Limit our aims?
• Lose sight of our impact?
• Quit too soon?
• Let our dreams fade?

All too often we hold ourselves back because we are intimidated by the depth and breadth of worthwhile causes that loom large on the big stage of life.

With ABT, the pursuit of your noble cause does not have to deflate or defeat you. It can be your lifeblood. It can wake you up, inspire you, and make you a better person – more competent, more fulfilled. **When you call yourself to action in this way, others instinctively want to join you.**

Let not thy will roar when thy power can but whisper.

THOMAS FULLER

CHANGE
THE WAY YOU
SEE
POWER

POWER

CONVENTIONAL WISDOM

- Knowledge and expertise
- Material wealth
- Authority
- Status and fame

CONVENTIONAL VIEWS OF POWER: WHAT YOU HAVE

When it comes to power, most people think of accumulating material wealth, status, authority, knowledge, and expertise. These are potent external sources of power. As such, they provide you with control over a vast array of resources - from money, to land, to market share, to intellectual property. While building large reservoirs of external power may be useful, it is not enough for getting results. There is another source of power equally important and often more vital to your leadership and your success.

ABT INSIGHTS

- Unique talents and strengths
- Passionate pursuits
- Values and beliefs
- Mission and purpose

ABT PERSPECTIVES ON POWER: WHO YOU ARE

Instead of relying primarily on external power sources to fuel your progress, look deeply inside for what can move you forward. You have a huge reservoir of internally generated power just waiting to be tapped. Internal sources of power derive from who you are – not what you have. Your internal power is defined by your Signature Presence – your unique combination of passions, capabilities, qualities, values, and beliefs. Signature Presence power gives you what it takes to get results when externally derived power is not enough.

THE WORLD BELONGS TO THOSE WHO SHOW UP

Woody Allen was on the right track when he said, "Eighty percent of life is just showing up."

Showing up is a straightforward act, but it's **HOW** you show up that makes all the difference…

and that is not as simple as it sounds. Showing up emphatically can feel awkward at first…

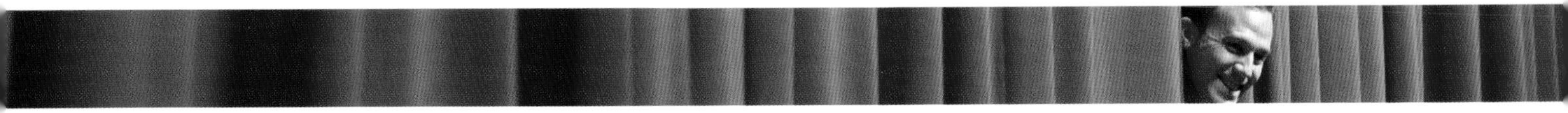

oo bold, even over the top. It takes intention, practice, and a bit of bravado. Each of us has to find and

develop our own way of "showing up." The way you show up will influence everything else that follows.

Showing up, as only you can, is a powerful asset for making an impact in all aspects of your life.

Just think about all the ways people show up and make their "presence" known. From bursting in the door to quietly slipping into the back of the room, from entering with a swagger to blending in, from slipping a note under the door to sending a singing telegram … there is no one way to show up. But there is one right way that's perfect for you and you alone. Remember, in ABT terms that's your Signature Presence … once you step into it and step out with it, your impact will grow exponentially.

Great Beginnings

Think back to a time when you have shown up confident and competent, right from the start. What were the circumstances?

- Making a new acquaintance?
- Coaching a colleague?
- Presenting a new idea?
- Solving a problem?
- Hosting a dinner party?
- Leading a discussion?

Pick one at a time. Slow down. Relive the experience fully. Savor it. Relish it. Dwell in the details of that moment. See the dominant colors, the features of your surroundings. Picture who else was present. Relive the important parts of conversations. How were you feeling?

What were you thinking? What did you say? Study your tone of voice, your body posture, stance, rhythm, gestures. Replay this memory in slow motion several times. Let the experience sink in until it really speaks to you. Until it's almost as vivid as actually being there. This memory will serve you well. An asset that anchors you in a moment when you – all of you – showed up. You were present, vital, on purpose. This is where your truest power comes from. Times when you show up as the truest version of yourself – your all-out, unvarnished, no kidding presence.

Get that.
Be that.
Do that.

Glimpse Your Signature Presence

What other person in your life truly knows you – the real, amazingly unique you? Your grandmother? Your spouse? Your colleague? Your highschool friend? Your college roommate? What stands out to those who know you best? How would they describe your talents and strengths? Ask them. Guess what they would say. Can you even imagine that you are one of a kind? **Your Signature Presence is your greatest asset.** Get a glimpse – now.

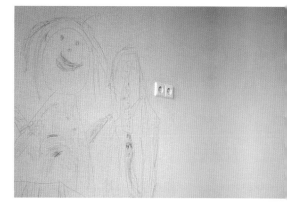

TRY THIS:

Take note of the assets that make you unique. List 5 assets that you possess (and can access no matter what.) Five is enough – more than enough to form your Signature Presence. Reflect on your personal asset profile. Watch yourself shift, light up, come alive. Keep exploring your view of your asset profile. Refine this profile of your Signature Presence as you gather more assets.

STAND FOR SOMETHING...
IT'S YOUR
PERSONAL PLATFORM

Leadership sage Warren Benis once said, "A point of view is worth 50 IQ points." He knew that when you live by the power of your convictions you stand taller, sit straighter, and speak more confidently. You raise the level of your game. Others know you as "a force of nature" – someone who will not be deterred and who doesn't give up.

- People crave clarity … your voice rings clear when you stand for something.
- People want wisdom … your mind creates meaning when you stand for something.
- People gravitate toward hope … your ideas and promises hold sway when you stand for something.

Create personal platforms to advance your important causes and agendas. Each Personal Platform should reflect the values and passions that underlie your beliefs. Let it declare your point of view … reveal what matters to you …and it will call others to action. Write, speak, and visualize the personal manifesto that boldly expresses where you stand. Don't be afraid of making "my" and "I" statements.

I believe…   My hope…

I want…   My desire…

I declare…   My dream…

"I" and "my" are powerful words that communicate and deliver your character and commitment.

Taking a Stand That Stands the Test of Time:

Your Personal Platform: Once articulated, it gives you solid ground on which to stand. It infuses your opinions and actions. It provides a filter through which to see the personal platforms of others. You know instantly if someone is speaking and acting in consort with deeply held beliefs that mesh with yours. Examples of well-articulated personal platforms abound and surround us.

· Commencement Addresses
· OpEd Letters
· Eulogies
· Political Campaigns

Seek them out. Be inspired.

Personal Platform Essays:

In 1951, radio pioneer Edward R. Murrow invited Americans from all walks of life to write essays about their most deeply held beliefs. In the aftermath of WWII and the earlier years of the Cold War, Murrow believed that these essays would help people see more deeply into the heart of American values. He was right.

Murrow's "This I Believe" essay series transcended all boundaries and barriers and enabled his listeners to rally around a set of shared beliefs.

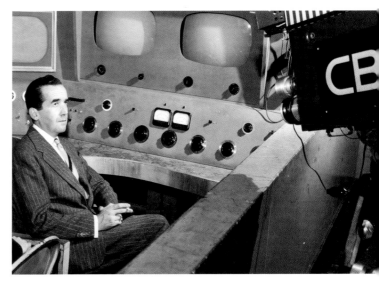

GENERAL
DOUGLAS McARTHUR
McArthur's devotion to
his country and the men
and women he led was
legendary. Let this excerpt
from McArthur's farewell
speech to the cadets at his
beloved West Point inspire
you to define your personal
platform.

Duty, Honor, Country: Those three hallowed words reverently dictate what you ought to be, what you can be, what you will be. They are your rallying points: to build courage when courage seems to fail; to regain faith when there seems to be little cause for faith; to create hope when hope becomes forlorn.

The soldier, above all other men, is required to practice the greatest act of religious training – sacrifice.
You are the leaven which binds together the entire fabric of our national system of defense … The Long Gray Line has never failed us. Were you to do so, a million ghosts in olive drab, in brown khaki, in blue and gray, would rise from their white crosses thundering those magic words: Duty, Honor, Country.

This does not mean that you are war mongers. On the contrary, the soldier, above all other people, prays for peace, for he must suffer and bear the deepest wounds and scars of war … You now face a new world – a world of change reaching out for a new and boundless frontier.

The shadows are lengthening for me. The twilight is here. My days of old have vanished, tone and tint. They have gone glimmering through the dreams of things that were. Their memory is one of wondrous beauty, watered by tears, and coaxed and caressed by the smiles of yesterday. I listen vainly, but with thirsty ears, for the witching melody of faint bugles blowing reveille, of far drums beating the long roll. In my dreams I hear again the crash of guns, the rattle of musketry, the strange, mournful mutter of the battlefield.

But in the evening of my memory, always I come back to West Point.

Always there echoes and re-echoes: Duty, Honor, Country.

Today marks my final roll call with you, but I want you to know that when I cross the river my last conscious thoughts will be of The Corps, and The Corps, and The Corps.

I bid you farewell.

NOW IT'S YOUR TURN!

Create your personal platform.

See who shows up.

Take Your Stand.

No matter what your cause, status, or life stage, the act of articulating your Personal Platform releases a rich reservoir of power. For most of us, the crafting process can be intimidating or daunting, but well worth the effort. You will feel more powerful almost immediately. Here are some simple ABT Personal Platform guidelines to help you.

Focus. Be bold.

Select a specific topic that reveals your deeply held beliefs. Create 5 declarations that begin with "I believe _____ about _____." Be clear and concrete. Don't hold back. State your beliefs in vivid, unequivocal terms that will be provocative and motivating.

Remember signature moments.

Reflect on pivotal moments that helped shape your beliefs about your topic. These pivotal moments could be interactions with family members, mentors, or teachers, or insights and emotional awakenings gained by reading about or witnessing events.

Get personal.

Tell personal stories that describe how these beliefs show up in your everyday life. Be specific and sensory. Describe the internal impact of your beliefs on what you say and do and on what others say and do in response.

Write. Edit. Hone.

Articulate your personal platform as an essay or "manifesto." Use your own words as you would actually speak them. Weave together your "I Believe" statements with your personal story.

Deliver it.

Read your Personal Platform out loud. Record it. Play it back. Feel it. Believe it.

BE AUTHENTIC
BY DEMAND

In everyday parlance, the word "demand" refers to harsh – even coercive – power that insists, pushes, and cajoles. In the language of the theater, however, "demand" has a very different connotation.

From the stage, to have "demand" means to possess the power to captivate and capture the minds and hearts of the audience. An actor with "demand" is so magnetic that the audience cannot resist their gaze, their voice, or their energy.

The actor's message and meaning are so engaging that the audience is no longer watching the actor perform. Instead, the audience is experiencing the actor's reality.

Whatever happens inside the actor happens inside the audience.

The secret to cultivating the irresistible, magnetic, theatrical brand of demand is to thoroughly embody your message. That's right – feel your message through your body. Remember, speaking and writing are physical actions. Join forces with your whole body as you would a musical instrument.

Find that soulful place deep inside where the fire in your belly can fuel what you are saying. Finding your voice energizes your message and magnetizes your power.

With singing, the name
of the game is to make
yourself believable.
When somebody hears
you sing a song and they
say, "Oh, that must have
happened to him," that's
when you know you're
transmitting. It's like
being a good actor.
You make people feel
things, emotions, and
whatnot. But you gotta
start with yourself.
You got to feel it yourself.

RAY CHARLES

Recall a time when someone's spoken message touched you, riveted your attention, resonated with you. What were the vocal and visceral qualities that moved you? What made the message irresistible? Compelling?

How could you incorporate these elements of demand into how and what you say? How can you give more voice to your beliefs? Put your heart into what you say. Savor the sounds. Let each word land and linger longer.

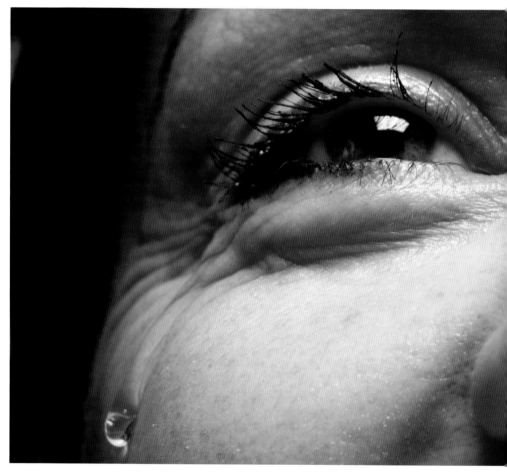

EXPOSE YOURSELF

When you reveal who you are... your values, passions, regrets, doubts, and dreams ... you become authentic, genuine, real. The more transparent you are about your personal experiences – the "good" and admirable alongside the "bad" and embarrassing – the more people will trust you, identify with you, and want to be around you.

You have probably been taught to believe that your personal power is bolstered only by the best of who you are and what you have accomplished. Conventional wisdom such as "put your best foot forward," "show them what you are made of," and "let them see your good side" is sound advice. However, it is only half of the story. Exposing the real, most vulnerable parts of yourself is counterintuitive.

As soon as you start admitting mistakes, it's natural for confusion and agonizing doubts to creep in. It's easy for a downward spiral to start.

However, with the right ABT mindset and a little perseverance, you will be able to see right through those doubts. You begin to see that your vulnerabilities are among your most valuable personal assets.

Your shortcomings and flaws actually increase your personal power exponentially when you reveal them for the sake of setting an example, righting a wrong, or accomplishing a greater good.

Dear JetBlue Customers,

We are sorry and embarrassed. But most of all, we are deeply sorry.

Last week was the worst operational week in JetBlue's seven year history. Many of you were either stranded, delayed or had flights cancelled following the severe winter ice storm in the Northeast. The storm disrupted the movement of aircraft, and, more importantly, disrupted the movement of JetBlue's pilot and inflight crewmembers who were depending on those planes to get them to the airports where they were scheduled to serve you. With the busy President's Day weekend upon us, rebooking opportunities were scarce and hold times at 1-800-JETBLUE were unusually long or not even available, further hindering our recovery efforts.

Words cannot express how truly sorry we are for the anxiety, frustration and inconvenience that you, your family, friends and colleagues experienced. This is especially saddening because JetBlue was founded on the promise of bringing humanity back to air travel, and making the experience of flying happier and easier for everyone who chooses to fly with us. We know we failed to deliver on this promise last week.

We are committed to you, our valued customers, and are taking immediate corrective steps to regain your confidence in us. We have begun putting a comprehensive plan in place to provide better and more timely information to you, more tools and resources for our crewmembers and improved procedures for handling operational difficulties. Most importantly, we have published the JetBlue Airways Customer Bill of Rights – our official commitment to you of how we will handle operational interruptions going forward – including details of compensation. We invite you to learn more at jetblue.com/promise.

You deserved better – a lot better – from us last week and we let you down. Nothing is more important than regaining your trust and all of us here hope you will give us the opportunity to once again welcome you onboard and provide you the positive JetBlue Experience you have come to expect from us.

Sincerely,
David Neeleman, *Founder and CEO*

SPEAK WITH SUBSTANCE, SIZZLE, & SOUL...

For most people, speaking is like breathing. We do it naturally. It comes easily. It is necessary and vital to living life. We thrive on conversations and interactions of all types. Speaking becomes exciting, energetic, and a source of power when you place yourself in the "showing up" frame of mind. You then instinctively realize that whenever you speak, you owe it to yourself to do so with purpose. You want to have a certain impact. Speaking in a way that reflects your Signature Presence is one of your most compelling assets and a potent form of power. Learn to use it wisely. Think of the power of speech as a combination of three basic assets:

Asset #1: Substance

The content of WHAT you say (e.g., facts, ideas, formulas, directions, strategies, etc.)

Asset #2: Sizzle

HOW you engage people (e.g., your tone, pauses, volume, resonance, interaction); HOW you craft what you say (e.g., stories, metaphors, analogies)

Asset #3: Soul

WHO you are (e.g., your passions, desires, aspirations, and values) and WHY your message is important to you

YOUR 93% ADVANTAGE

Most people spend the majority of their preparation time on the substance of what they want to communicate. Unfortunately substance accounts for only about 7% of why people will remember and believe in what you say.

Communication research reveals that the elements of sizzle and soul pack the most power into your impact ... on the order of 93%.

People remember what you say when you provide stories with vivid sensory detail (sizzle). People believe you and trust you when they can see that your message is important to you on the deepest level (soul). People assess your integrity and credibility when you speak. Listeners have Geiger counters for authenticity.

When something is worth saying, when the stakes are high, when you want to use yourself and your personal power to your best advantage, remember to include "sizzle" and "soul." Before you speak, ask yourself these powerful questions:

> What is my message in one sentence?
> — (SUBSTANCE)

> How will I engage? Entertain? Make my message memorable?
> — (SIZZLE)

> Why is this so important to me? Why am I saying what I am saying?
> — (SOUL)

As audience members we know if we like the speaker or not in the first 20 seconds. You do not have 5 minutes to warm up. If you have not grabbed the audience before you begin to speak, you have a lot of catching up to do.

GIFFORD BOOTH

MAP YOUR LIFE –
LOVE YOUR STORY

Meet Your Purpose,

Passion, and Potential

for the First Time …

All Over Again.

The ultimate way to unleash the power of your Signature Presence is to see yourself in action across your life-span. This gives you a powerful form of self-awareness that helps you bring your whole, best self forward into the present and the future.

When you examine how the episodes and events of your life have unfolded and how key moments have shaped you – your Signature Presence will shine through.

You can discern which

forces have shaped you

into the unique, talented

person you are.

When you scan the phases of your life retrospectively, looking for who and what had the greatest impact on you, the story of your life begins to tell itself. The story illuminates nuances and subtleties about you that you never noticed while they were happening.

With the benefit of this type of selective attention you can see even the most familiar aspects of your life in a whole new way. Your story crafts itself from the memories and imaginations of your Signature Experiences – experiences that engraved themselves in you. Your story is like a mirror and an X-ray at the same time.

It reflects who you are as a

whole person and feature

by feature as well.

Examining the story of your life "up to the moment" illuminates the foundation of your purpose, passion, and potential. It gives you laser vision into the unique core of who you are and what you were "born to do."

Your ABT Life Map

If you are like most people, creating a map of your life will be a new experience. The approach you take should be filled with the kind of curiosity and energy that children have at play.

Assemble pens, pencils, colored markers, and paper long enough to make a time line in 5-year increments, from your birth to your current age (shelf paper about 3 feet long works well). You can also do this Reflection Exercise online at www.assetbasedthinking.com. Try it both ways.

Create your ABT Life Map. Identify the key experiences and people that have shaped and molded you (e.g., turning points, peaks, valleys, crossroads, mentors, allies, even enemies). Reflect on what you have

made happen and what has happened to make you "YOU". Chronicle the **Signature Experiences of your life** with words or symbols to signify the type of impact each event has made. Use stars, exclamation points, question marks, happy, mad, or sad faces. Be creative. Express yourself – surprise yourself. As you remember and map the Signature Experiences of your life, your Signature Presence will come into sharper focus. Be sure to include life-shaping events that were outside of your direct control (e.g., calamities, windfalls, disappointments, and blessings). Note the assets you used to cope with or leverage what happened. Note which assets emerged in the process. Give yourself one hour to work on the first draft of your ABT Life Map. This is enough time to capture the highlights and low lights.

Do the same for the events of your life that you were able to influence (e.g., mistakes, successes, achievements, failures). Inventory the assets you developed in these instances.

After 50 minutes or so, start looking for patterns in your assets. Notice which ones fit together into categories. Discover and name at least five robust categories of assets that define who you are. Maybe you see patterns of optimism, resilience, compassion, decisiveness, or creativity. Maybe you see a sense of humor, truthfulness, dedication, or leadership emerging from the story of your life adventure.

These asset categories give you a glimpse into who you are and what you have to offer. Life Mapping gives you a refreshingly clear and incisive glimpse of your Signature Presence. Next, look at the patterns in the events themselves. Ask yourself how the events both

outside of your direct control and under your direct influence have been beneficial to you. See all the ways you have grown and advanced. How have you honed your skills, capabilities, and character?

Most importantly, note the patterns in what you strive for, what attracts you, and what is attracted to you. What captures your committed attention? These patterns offer you insight and foresight into your raison d'être – why you are. Your mighty causes reveal themselves right before your very eyes.

BRADFORD WG LIBRARY
100 HOLLAND COURT, BOX 130
BRADFORD, ONT. L3Z 2A7

Revisit your ABT Life Map often over the next weeks, months, and years. Let it teach, guide, and inspire you. Share it with others you trust and value. Ask what they see. Ask them what surprises or amazes them about the life you are leading. Other people will see assets in you that you don't see. Believe them.

Edit or add to your map as your perspective sharpens. Let your Signature Presence and your raison d'être speak their mind. Listen. You will find your view of yourself shifting. You will feel a sense of pride, confidence, and energy. You will be fortified by a bigger, better view of yourself. The ABT view of you inspires you to have influence and impact and live the adventure you were born to have.

What lies behind you and what lies in front of you pale in comparison to what lies inside of you.

RALPH WALDO EMERSON

We mark with light in the memory the few interviews we have had with souls that made our souls wiser, that spoke what we thought, that told us what we knew, to leave us be what only we are.

RALPH WALDO EMERSON

CHANGE
THE WAY YOU
SEE
INFLUENCE

INFLUENCE

CONVENTIONAL WISDOM

- Change others' minds
- Debate
- Compete
- Prevail

CONVENTIONAL VIEWS OF INFLUENCE: **MY INFLUENCE**

To be influential is to win over the minds, hearts, spirits, and efforts of other people. Conventionally, our view of how to become influential is focused on developing our personal influence skills. Our emphasis is on persuading, convincing, advocating, and winning the argument so we can get people on our side. While this approach to influencing others is effective, it is not the only approach – and very often not the best.

IN PART TWO, YOU WILL LEARN HOW TO HONE YOUR OWN INFLUENCE SKILLS AND EXPAND THE INFLUENCE THAT EMANATES FROM THE QUALITY AND DIVERSITY OF YOUR RELATIONSHIPS.

ABT INSIGHTS

- Change your mind
- Dialogue
- Admire
- Engage

ABT PERSPECTIVES ON INFLUENCE: OUR INFLUENCE

Forming robust networks of committed relationships is the hallmark of ABT influence. With ABT, influence is mutual and reciprocal. With ABT you put the opinions, desires, interests, and passions of others on a par with your own. You make *being influenced* as important as *being influential*.

IT'S NOT JUST WHO YOU KNOW, IT'S HOW YOU KNOW THEM

You've often heard the adage "it's who you know" that matters. Knowing the right people can certainly make a positive difference when it comes to getting into the best colleges or clubs, landing a plum job or a promotion, or scoring a good table at a hot restaurant. Having "good connections" does help make you more influential but it plays only a minor role.

Influence is a two-way street

Asset-Based Thinking helps you connect with "people in the know" more deeply and authentically. With ABT you embrace the fact that influence is a two-way street by acknowledging the assets you are giving and the assets you are getting in every interaction. This takes your ability to influence – your Influence Quotient – to a whole new level.

Your ABT Influence Quotient

- More people are drawn to you
- You are drawn to more people
- You recognize and celebrate others out loud
- You persuade others and let others persuade you
- Your relationships are mutually rewarding

- Your "circles of influence" multiply

Circles of Influence:
Expand them by making others the center of your attention:

With Asset-Based Thinking, you realize that how you know another person – how deeply, how respectfully, how truthfully – directly influences how they in turn know you. It spells the difference between fleeting attraction and loyal allegiance. With ABT you instinctively and inquisitively focus on others. You pay attention to how they "show up." You probe and investigate the minds and hearts of everyone you encounter to get to know them for who they are.

Lead with questions, search for assets:

1. What do they value? Believe in?
2. What are they thinking? Feeling?
3. What else do they want? Need? Aspire to?
4. What can I do to recognize them?
5. What can I offer them?
6. How can I serve them?
7. What can they offer to my cause?

Never doubt that a small band of committed citizens can changed the world. It's the only thing that ever has.

MARGARET MEAD

TRY THIS:

ABT Networking for 7 Days

Make a list of people in your circles:
- Name 3 people you love and admire
- 2-3 people you feel neutral toward
- 1-2 who usually annoy or frustrate you

For 7 days, every time you encounter one of these people, step inside their interests, desires, and concerns by letting any of these questions be front and center in your mind. Pick the ones that will meaningfully expand your understanding of them and will deepen your connection, trust, and empathy.

Experience how your relationships shift and improve with the entire range of those you selected ... even those in your "annoying" category.

Remember, when you lead with an ABT question you see and embrace what is true in others and what is important to them. It changes how you know them in one conversation. Your "Circles of Influence" widen and deepen – one conversation at a time.

EMBRACE

MAKE "EYE"-TO-"I" CONTACT

Among the tribes of Northern Natal in South Africa, there is a customary exchange when two people pass each other casually on the street:

Greeting:

Sawu bona
"I am seen."

Response:

Sikhona
"I am here."

This simple exchange reflects a profound truth: a person must be "seen" (acknowledged) to be fully present to another. When you truly see with your eyes the "I" of someone's essence, that person feels valued.

Think of how often you interact with people and never actually look at them. At the dry cleaners, in the coffee shop, passing in the hallway – encounters are fleeting and people go unnoticed. You can, however, use these brief interactions as "practice fields" to hone your ABT skills for those situations that matter most.

Next time, really see the person.

Why not benefit from the Natal tradition of acknowledgment as a more powerful genuine way of greeting that person? Notice what the person is wearing, facial features, expressions, and mannerisms that are attractive and special. Allow yourself to be interested and curious about what there is to like or admire.

Stay open. Go beyond eye contact to "I" connection.

STAY OPEN

Recognition is the greatest motivator.

GERARD C. EAKEDALE

Turn off the multitasking switch.
Be present.

This isn't easy in today's world of 24-7 connectivity, text messaging, and Blackberry addictions. When you approach even a casual conversation with the intention of making an "Eye-to-I" connection, the other person will almost always reciprocate. Mirroring the level of connection and interest offered is a natural human tendency. This is a basic, hard-wired asset you can count on.

Recent findings in social neuroscience reveal that face-to-face, eye-to-eye connections form a kind of physiological closed feedback loop.

When two people make meaningful, sustained eye contact during a conversation, the neural networks in the occipital frontal cortex (OFC) of each person's brain begin to fire in synchrony. This is the neuro-physiological equivalent of having a rapport with and genuinely feeling connected to someone. In fact scientists have dubbed the neurons that mimic one another "mirror neurons." Your ability to influence increases exponentially when your brain physiology is in sync with another's.

Socially intelligent leadership starts with being fully present and getting in sync. Once a leader is engaged the full panoply of social intelligence can come into play.

DANIEL GOLEMAN

TRY THIS:

See to Get in Sync

When you want to influence someone, get in sync first. For three consecutive days, practice getting in sync in real time. Focus on seeing, connecting, valuing, and appreciating others right there on the spot.

In casual conversation over dinner, during business meetings or family gatherings, notice how long it takes to get in sync. Feel the rapport build. Make that first small move to influence. Watch what happens. With ABT, small shifts in "sync" can make seismic differences in influence.

RAPPORT

LISTEN SOFTER

You have most likely heard the statement, "Listen harder." Teachers, parents, coaches, and mentors say this when they want you to pay closer attention and take a message in. You probably say it to yourself sometimes as a way of focusing and blocking out distractions. "Listening harder" implies narrowing your focus into an almost laser-like beam that zeros in on what a person is saying.

A more rewarding form of listening is to "Listen softer." Soft listening implies showering your attention on someone in a way that illuminates the deeper significance of what is being said. To listen softer you must widen the lens of what catches your attention by listening with your eyes and heart. By listening softer the distance between listener and speaker fades. The soft listener's awareness dissolves into the other person's presence and you both hear and feel more.

LISTEN
HARDER

Be a quick change artist:

In the award-winning off-Broadway play "No Child," actress Nilaja Sun plays the part of many diverse characters: the school principal, teachers, a janitor, and rebellious teenagers from a public school in the Bronx. Like magic, Sun becomes a pregnant Latina schoolgirl, then fades seamlessly into the 60-year-old arthritic African American janitor, Joe.

She emerges next as a frightened, Russian-immigrant substitute teacher right before your eyes. For over two hours, Nilaja Sun performs a monologue montage of voices, bodies, and personalities so distinct from one another that her feat of becoming each character seems impossible. In rave reviews, Sun is referred to as a "quick change artist."

Sun does all this by "listening softer." So softly that she is able to penetrate the heart, mind, body, and soul of each person she portrays. She transcends the boundaries between herself and the other by evaporating the distinctions.

She lets go of who she is in favor of embodying the other.

"No Child" is an amazing example of the degree of empathy that is possible between people when you truly open yourself up.

Feeling the pain, passion, delight, and moods of another creates mutually empathetic feelings of freedom and safety. Each person feels so seen, so known, that no inhibition or hiding is required. Both people show up in full fashion. Resistance evaporates and permission to influence emerges.

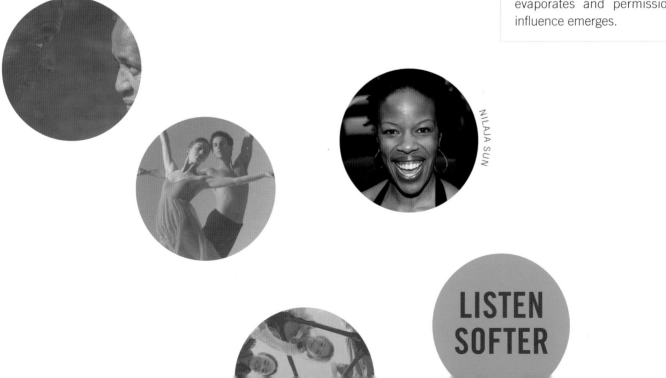

NILAJA SUN

LISTEN SOFTER

Trade Places

Replay three recent conversations
in your mind in this order:

 1 One that was exciting, upbeat,
and rewarding.

 2 One that was ordinary, transac-
tional, just-doing-business.

3 One that was frustrating,
and irritating – even tense
or argumentative.

In each, view things from the other person's perspective. See what that person saw. Think their thoughts, feel their feelings, step into their shoes. Remember what they said. Imagine what else they could have said. Adopt each person's point of view.

Notice how:
• Fully you can inhabit the other person's point of view
• Your interest, empathy, compassion, and admiration for the person grow

Let no man imagine that he has no influence. Whoever he may be, and wherever he may be placed, the man who thinks becomes a light and a power.

HUMBERTO MATURANA

EXCHANGE

GIVE TRUTH
THE UPPER HAND

Influence requires truth. Truth deepens and enhances your influence.

Whether circumstances are positive or negative, whether the news is good or bad, people want the truth from you. Truth is often relative. Your "truth" may be different from mine. Remember, the truth is synonymous with your integrity. Once spoken it is powerful and profound.

With truth you can change minds, win confidence, and move people to action. People crave hearing the truth and knowing exactly what they are facing. Truth is the foundation of trust between leaders and followers, husbands and wives, friends and coworkers. Trust founded on the truth means "You can believe me" and "I can believe you."

INTEGRITY

Seek not greatness, but seek truth and you will find both.

HORACE MANN

Give truth a voice

When you speak the truth about how you feel and what you think, others see you more clearly. The more transparent you are, the more trustworthy and influential you become.

Start by emphasizing the truth
about what you admire, like, and value.

Expressing what is truly good is the foundation for truth telling. In fact, when you tell the truth by expressing your appreciation, or celebrating a success out loud, or recognizing outstanding achievements, people become more open and receptive to you. They bask in the glory of your praise. You build trust and your power to influence fastest when you start emphasizing the truth about what you admire, like, and value.

DESMOND TUTU

My humanity is bound up in yours, for we can only be human together.

91

Tell the Best Truth First

Be on the lookout for the truth: Notice what someone is contributing, what efforts are most effective, what qualities make that person special, unique, valuable. Then speak what you believe to be true.

Tell the person

What I appreciate/value/admire about you and what you did is
_____ .

The positive impact on me was
_____ .

The positive impact on others was _____ .

Search for what's right and what's working.

Combine expressing the best of what you see in others with the best truth about events and circumstances. Scan for what's moving in the right direction. Speak up to signify progress and opportunities. Being a spokesperson for advancements encourages optimism, creates hope, and builds resilience and momentum in any endeavor.

Tell what is true and best by stating:

We can make the most of this opportunity by _____.

The positive impacts on all of us involved are _____.

The positive impacts on our challenge/goal are _____.

Motivation is everything. You can do the work of two people, but you can't be two people. Instead, you have to inspire the next guy down the line and get him to inspire his people.

LEE IACOCCA

HONEST

93

Asset-Based Thinking offers a better way of telling the truth when it's hard to say and hard to hear.

When you hear the phrase, "to be perfectly honest," this usually implies "I am going to tell you the whole truth (not a half truth), no matter how hard it might be to hear."

This phrase reflects how hard it is to give truthful feedback that might offend someone or hurt their feelings. Yet people do appreciate constructive feedback if it's offered out of genuine concern for their best interest and from a belief that they are capable and competent.

Have Courageous Conversations

Use Asset-Based Thinking to give constructive feedback that could help another person change for the better. Courageous conversations strengthen relationships by navigating skillfully through a difficult interaction. Take all the time you need to formulate your messages. Then, tell the truth fast.

Use ABT to foster speedy resolutions and diffuse negative reactions by following these three steps. Be sure to formulate and rehearse the conversation to start and end positively.

> *If you tell the truth, you don't have to remember anything.*
>
> MARK TWAIN

1

Mentally list 3 to 5 qualities that you value (or even admire) about the person that are independent of the irritating behavior. This creates a more balanced view.

2

State the behavior that concerns you clearly and concisely. Then state the impact of that behavior on you and the relationship.

3

Present your positive vision of what is possible. Ask the person to join you to resolve the issue.

The positive note you end on will set the tone for the rest of the conversation. Then, relax and listen closely for the solution in whatever the other person says next.

VALUE

EARN
A STANDING
OVATION

Bill Strickland is the founder of a Philadelphia-based culinary arts program for delinquent, truant teenage boys. And does he know how to influence an audience! Every time he speaks, he gets a standing ovation (followed by big donations of time and money for his cause).

Why is Bill Strickland so moving and motivating? How does he attract and compel people to his mighty cause? His stature? Maybe. (Bill is 6'6" tall and in great shape.) His story? Sure. (He quit his day job to found his school and reclaim the lives of boys who grew up in his old neighborhood.) His motivation? Absolutely. (He broke the cycle of crime, drugs, and poverty for younger generations.) His sense of humor? Of course. (Like any great entertainer, Bill makes sure that the audience laughs hard.) And, something else … along with the laughs, Bill also helps them feel sadness, pride, surprise.

BILL STRICKLAND

Assets Exposed = Ovations

Bill's assets – stature, motivation and sense of humor – are keys to his impact and his ability to get audiences on their feet. They are important, but not enough to command the kind of standing ovations that Bill always gets.

So how does he do it? Bill opens himself up and lets people see his mighty cause in action. His transparency taps into what everyone in the audience desires – to care enough and do enough to make a difference. The exuberance of seeing how Bill pursues his mighty cause lights a fire in each member of the audience.

Desire to have impact runs deep

So deep that it is sometimes silent, even asleep, in most people who are living their busy lives. Bill Strickland wakes up that desire. Through Bill, the audience reconnects with their own personal passion to make a positive impact. They rise and applaud what Bill has touched in themselves. That's right, they are giving themselves a standing ovation.

Standing ovations celebrate the possibilities

Follow Bill Strickland's lead. Make what you say and do to advance your mighty cause awaken other people's desire to join you. People long to operate in the domain of what is larger, bigger, more far-reaching than the confines of their everyday life and work. When you tap that deeper stream of desire in those you seek to influence, people will join you, volunteer their effort, and invest themselves.

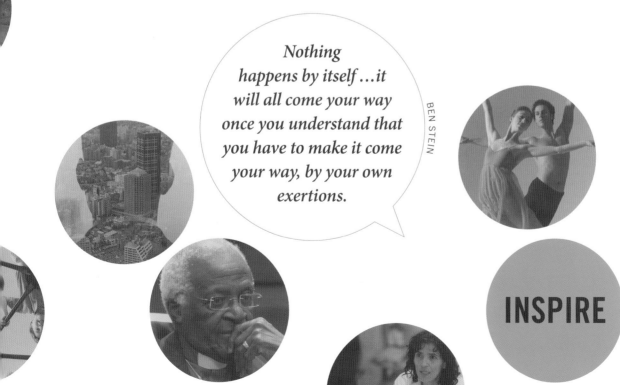

Nothing happens by itself …it will all come your way once you understand that you have to make it come your way, by your own exertions.

BEN STEIN

INSPIRE

Whether delivering a formal speech or having a casual conversation, you have the opportunity to influence and engage others. With the right preparation it becomes second nature to you. Speak to the deeper purpose of your cause. Make your call to action an invitation to others. Articulate how others can contribute. Communicate the personal and wider-world benefits. Your vision is perhaps the greatest gift you have to offer. An authentic and meaningful challenge, emotionally delivered,

Ask not what your country can do for you. Ask what you can do for your country.

JOHN F. KENNEDY

DREAM

brings people to their feet, moves them, attracts them, and launches concentrated effort. They become connected to you and what you have to say.

Express the deeper **meaning** and significance of your call to action in one powerful sentence that reveals your mighty cause. Ask others to join you. Tell them what they can do. How they can make a difference. Be inspired by memorable messages that earned standing ovations.

I have a dream that my four little children will one day live in a nation where they will not be judged by the color of their skin but by the content of their character.

MARTIN LUTHER KING, JR.

ADMIRE SOMEONE

What you admire in someone, you have in yourself. It may be only a glimmer, but it is there. In fact, when a person's talent, virtue, skill, or attitude strikes you as amazing, you can be sure it's something you want more of. When you embrace this truth you are ready, willing, and able to incorporate the admirable qualities of others into your repertoire of assets.

What you see is what you want to be.

That's why it's so important to be on the lookout for how others lead and build followings. How do they:
• Show up
• Influence
• Make their impact

ABT helps in two important ways. First, it teaches how to scan for what is amazing, incredible and worthwhile about leaders from all walks of life:

- The crossing guard
- The teacher
- The general
- The chef
- The mother
- The conductor
- The valedictorian
- The rabbi or priest
- The quarterback
- The nurse

Next, perhaps most importantly, you learn how to blend and integrate those qualities in yourself. Your asset inventory then transforms, expands, and deepens.

I have never been especially impressed by the heroics of people who are convinced they are about to change the world. I am more awed by those who struggle to make one small difference after another.

ELLEN GOODMAN

EMULATE

Images of Success

Make a list of leaders you admire. Those publicly prominent and those most personally relevant. Then reflect on their assets and qualities. Note the one who stands out the most. Make a list of what attracts you most in order of priority. Then choose the single asset

QUEEN NOOR

It is women who are the key to breaking out of poverty, breaking out of stagnation. It's women who can contribute to achieving real security – not bombs and bullets and repressive goverments.

If you want your life to be more rewarding, you have to change the way you think.

OPRAH WINFREY

MARGARET THATCHER

Look at a day when you are supremely satisfied at the end. It's not a day when you lounge around doing nothing; it's when you had everything to do and you've done it.

you are ready to cultivate in yourself and let it be your aspiration for one week. See and feel yourself expressing, demonstrating, and living that asset.

Be prepared for your influence to expand.

There is nothing like returning to a place that remains unchanged to find ways in which you yourself have altered.

NELSON MANDELA

One cannot and must not try to erase the past merely because it does not fit the present.

GOLDA MEIR

No one learns more about a problem than the person at the bottom.

SANDRA DAY O'CONNOR

History will be kind to me, for I intend to write it.

WINSTON CHURCHILL

You can never really live anyone else's life, not even your child's. The influence you exert is through your own life, and what you've become yourself.

ELEANOR ROOSEVELT

There is a boundary to men's passions when they act from feelings; but none when they are under the influence of imagination.

EDMUND BURKE

Far away there in the sunshine are my highest aspirations. I may not reach them, but I ca

*The secret of my
influence has
always been that it
remained secret.*

SALVADOR DALI

*Don't be afraid
to take a big step.
You can't cross
a chasm in two
small jumps.*

DAVID LLOYD GEORGE

*It takes tremendous
discipline to control
the influence, the
power you have over
other people's lives.*

CLINT EASTWOOD

ok up and see their beauty, believe in them, and try to follow where they lead.

LOUISA MAY ALCOTT

SAINT FRANCIS OF ASSISI

Start by do-ing what is necessary, then do what is possible, and suddenly you are doing the impos-sible.

— SAINT FRANCIS OF ASSISI

CHANGE
THE WAY YOU
SEE
IMPACT

IMPACT

CONVENTIONAL WISDOM

- External imperatives
- Gain control
- Advancement
- Solve problems

CONVENTIONAL VIEWS OF IMPACT: **WHAT THE WORLD WANTS**

When we think of having an impact, we usually think of doing something to satisfy the needs and requirements of the places where we live and work. We seek impacts that solve problems, remove threats, and advance the current status of what we know and know how to do. Asset-Based Thinking builds on this conventional wisdom by showing you how to connect what you want to make happen to what the wider world needs from you.

IN
PART
THREE YOU
WILL INTERACT
WITH ABT PRINCIPLES
AND PRACTICES THAT WILL
ENABLE YOU TO CREATE IMPACT
THAT IS BOTH PERSONALLY
FULFILLING AND IN
SERVICE OF THE
"GREATER
GOOD."

ABT INSIGHTS

- Internal imperatives
- Lose control
- Fulfillment
- Seize opportunities

ABT PERSPECTIVES ON IMPACT: WHAT I WANT TO MAKE HAPPEN

ABT impact starts with setting your sights on the results you want to make happen – on the visions that inspire and motivate you most. Generating personally meaningful visions to pursue helps you prioritize external demands and determine how you will respond to them. With ABT you also connect each of your personal visions to the mighty cause you feel born to serve. This dual focus creates momentum and a whole host of unexpected, beneficial outcomes.

THIS IS YOUR TIME. CLAIM IT!

Making an impact is rooted in what you were born to do. Your impact comes to life at the intersection of your present actions and the future you want to create. Impact comes in all shapes and sizes. Your impact may be starting a business, changing a law, raising teenagers, or reducing crime or illiteracy. Many people have multiple agendas. Most of us are attracted to more than one mighty cause in the course of a lifetime.

• Regardless of how broad or narrow your agenda, how many or how few your desires, the Asset-Based Thinking approach to making an impact is the same. The impact you seek in your outer world must be fueled by the assets of passion and purpose from your inner world. When the imperatives of your outer world and inner world intersect, you know that it is "your time." You are ready, willing and able to "claim it," own it, and run with it.

Your Signature Impact

Two key ABT Impact Perspectives
will help you achieve the future
you deserve and increase the
odds that your Signature Impact
will make a difference. Reflect on
each – then move forward with
purpose and passion.

BE THE CHANGE

ABT Impact Perspective #1:
People Trump Process
and Procedures

Impact means moving from the current reality to the future reality you desire. Being clear and specific about the future you seek and how it is better than the present is essential. When you think "impact" think "change."

Describe the changes in beliefs, attitudes, and behaviors required of you and those you intend to impact. This mind's-eye comparison creates a magnetic pull mechanism that propels you and others forward. You reach your destination in less time with energy to spare.

ABT Impact Perspective #2:
Your Enthusiasm Inspires Others to Passionate Action

The bigger the impact you seek, the bigger the shared effort that is required. Your ultimate impact is in direct proportion to the magnetic pull of your enthusiasm and passion for your mighty cause.

Enthusiasm sustains you (and others) during the ups and downs. Enthusiasm fuels determination and creativity and sparks hope and resilience. Best of all, it's contagious.

Don't make the mistake of going it alone. Build an enthusiastic core of positive conspirators from the very beginning. You can't miss.

MAKE DESIRE MORE IMPORTANT THAN FEAR

Recent findings in health care research show that fear of death does not motivate human beings to sustain healthier lifestyles. Even heart attack survivors will not change their lifestyle (e.g., stop smoking, start exercising, lose weight) when told they will die if they don't. Attention-getting scare tactics and fear of dying motivate only for a while – on the order of 90 days. Why? It turns out that the fear of death becomes so overwhelming that we put it out of our minds. And when we keep waking up in the morning, even when we didn't exercise the day before, the motivating power of fear diminishes.

Research confirms that when it comes to forming healthier lifestyle habits people respond to the **potential rewards**. The promise of achieving more energy, a better sex life, and increased happiness is what fuels sustainable changes in behaviors.

JUMP IN

ABT AXIOM: Focus on what you want (not avoiding what you don't want). Desire-driven goals stimulate motivation, build enthusiasm, and ignite the passion you need to define and achieve the future you most desire.

JACKIE ROBINSON

A life is not important except in the impact it has on other lives.

Better Ways for Better Days

Craft the vision of something you want to make happen. Your initial vision is a first draft. Then invite a core group of people (up to 5) who have a vested interest in your impact to help you shape your future vision from their perspective. Make them your advisors. Let them interview you about why this vision is so important to you. Have them ask you at least 3 times about why you want to make your vision happen. Define the changes your desired future requires. Changes in: • beliefs • attitudes • behaviors • processes • systems • infrastructure

This is the basic framework and support system you need to begin your quest for better "ways" and better "days." When you practice collaborating to create robust visions on a small scale … you enhance your ability to do so with larger-scale pursuits.

Note: Give yourself the gift of time and encouragement to define the forces of your mighty cause. Go back through the book. Note the wider-world agendas that caught your attention or ignited your passion. The worthy causes that matter most to you. The patterns of successes and challenges you highlighted in your life map may also provide some helpful insight. Ask yourself how your vision reflects your mighty cause.

Imagine. Dream. Envision the future you want.

Commit to something BIG. Apply ABT impact skills to attract others to your cause. Watch what happens. As you read the next story, be inspired by how Nancy Hult Ganis's vision, signature impact, and passion come together.

LAURENCE FISHBURNE & KEKE PALMER IN AKEELAH AND THE BEE

ABT Impact Story
Akeelah and the Bee: A Film That Shines a Light

Nancy Hult Ganis
Broadcast Journalist, Film Producer, Change Agent

Nancy Hult Ganis began her media career in public television almost 30 years ago and she has spent a good part of her life shining the light on inequities in education. It is her passion and personal platform. "I saw at a fairly early age that there were terrible inequities in the education system and I've always felt compelled to try to give back."

As an accomplished producer and broadcaster, Nancy is always looking for compelling stories to tell. She believes deeply in the power of the medium of film to inform people about social issues. "There was a motto in my children's school that has guided my work. 'If you hear you forget, if you see you remember, if you experience you understand.'"

One day in 2000 her husband Sid gave her a script to read, *Akeelah and the Bee:* a powerful story written by Doug Atchison about a South Los Angeles teenage girl with a very special aptitude, a gift for words, and an eagerness to realize her potential. "I read the script in one sitting. I said to my husband, 'We have

to make this. This is a way to bring so many things I care about to millions of viewers in an entertaining and emotional way.'"

Both the content of the film and the personal passion and perseverance it took to get it made are examples of ABT at its best. What is so impressive about Nancy is that she has deeply held beliefs and principles by which she lives, and she is committed to helping the rest of us "get it" and get with it. "This movie gives people a chance to experience children falling through the cracks and then see how, with the right conditions and support systems, they can turn out to be much more than anyone ever expected."

Akeelah and the Bee was released by Lions Gate in April of 2006 to rave reviews and was selected by Starbucks to be the first ever full-length feature film to be sold and marketed through their retail stores. The movie is also used as a motivational tool in classrooms around the country. The positive ripple effect of Nancy's pursuit of her mighty cause will be felt for generations to come. "When we recognize and give children the resources, the access, the contacts, the mentors, they need to be successful, they thrive. I think we all lose if we don't."

Visit www.akeelahandthebee.com and See the Light

ABT Impact Story
"Leadership Wins the Day"

In 2005, at age 48, Jim Spence was leading a division of a Fortune 100 company. The business was under pressure, market share and sales were dropping, and competitors were gaining momentum. His colleagues respected his intelligence and his determination to reverse the downward business trend. Jim was convinced that a shift in focus from problem solving to possibility generating would win the day. Jim also believed that it was his job to lead the way.

Jim was prepared. A year prior he had embarked on a leadership development path. He gathered detailed feedback about the pluses and minuses of his leadership style. Jim's colleagues valued his business acumen, drive, strategic thinking, and decision-making skills. They also sometimes felt intimidated and de-energized by his tendency to judge and criticize people for failing to meet his expectations. Jim's leadership assets were strong. But so were his leadership gaps.

He was up for the challenge of change. Jim began by framing his gaps as aspirations, not problems. He formulated three goals:

1)
Celebrate and recognize others when they succeed.
2)
Inspire and coach others to forge ahead when they fail.
3)
Turn the business challenges into an opportunity.

This simple shift from problem-focused DBT to possibility-focused ABT made Jim feel more powerful because he was striving for a personal win, a new mind-set, and a new skill set.

People in his organization began to feel more valued and worked harder. They emulated Jim's ABT management style and almost immediately productivity and morale improved. Jim's leadership had measurable impacts on results. One year later, market share and sales were rising, the business had regained its leadership position, and growth opportunities had returned. As a bonus, the work environment exuded optimism and energy instead of skepticism and lethargy.

Jim's desire to lead more effectively by appealing to the desires (not fears) of his colleagues won the day. He was later promoted to vice president of a larger business. Now he's applying more of the same in a new and even bigger role.

TRY THIS:

Start Small, Win Fast

When your desired impact requires attitude or behavior change, start small to win fast. For example, when you want others to be more proactive, notice even the slightest shifts in the right direction. Call attention to what you see. Praise new behavior. Ask people to describe the benefit of being more energetic and taking more initiative. The greatest persuader of all is personal experience.

LEAD

Find more ABT impact stories and send in yours to www.assetbasedthinking.com

The reasonable man adapts himself to the conditions that surround him. The unreasonable man adapts surrounding conditions to himself. All progress depends on the unreasonable man.

GEORGE BERNARD SHAW

HERMANN HESSE

I have always believed, and I still believe, that whatever good or bad fortune may come our way we can always give it meaning and transform it into something of value.

LOSE CONTROL...
GAIN GROUND

BE COMMITTED

Your Skin in the Game

When you pursue your mighty cause and personal visions it's natural to want to be in charge. After all, it's your vision! Instinctively you want to hold yourself 100% responsible and accountable. With that much skin in the game, it is tempting to want control over all the variables.

Control vs. Commitment

Striving for control is tempting, yet ultimately defeating. Instead of being in constant control, concentrate on being steadfastly committed. Then you gain ground either by being in the driver's seat or by giving someone else the wheel.

Positive Paradox

Think of the path to your future as a dance between who and what is in charge. Sometimes you take the lead over opposing forces – sometimes those opposing forces lead you. On your adventure, you can be sure that you will encounter opposing forces … ABT prepares you to make the most of them. And don't forget that you will meet positive forces along the way. ABT helps you let go so those forces propel you forward.

Make Opposition Your Ally

What characterisitics do Americans admire most in others? Power? Wealth? Attractiveness? Fame? A national polling firm conducted a study that reveals it is the "ability to overcome adversity." Intuitively you know that if a person can meet adversity with courage and creativity, that person is more likely to succeed in most aspects of life. So, when you encounter opposition and adversity, let ABT help you triumph by making opposition your ally. Here's how ...

Step 1

See more, more often: Remember the children's picture games? "Find 8 items hidden in a seemingly straightforward picture." At first, you are stumped ... then, upon closer examination, you see the things that were hidden at first glance. You can employ these same search skills to spot the opportunities in adversity. Look into the nuances of frustrating situations to find the gold. For example, see your motivation to land a better job after losing one. Discover what you didn't know after making a mistake. Notice how loyal you are when someone lets you down.

Step 2

Calculate what you've lost: Fine-tune your assessment of the downsides. Consider only significant setbacks. This will help you gain an accurate perspective.

Sometimes your losses are less serious than you thought. **The important thing is that you practice positive "damage control" as the precursor to "opportunity expansion."**

Step 3

Dig deep for potential gains: Now get optimistic. When you estimate the gains that could result from dealing with upheaval, the mind-set of possibility takes over. Mine the gold by looking for the upsides. Ask others what they see as potential gains.

Step 4

Rig your results: Now tally up the losses and the gains. Make sure the gains outweigh the losses. It's not "cheating" to "stack the deck" in your favor. Keep looking for ways you can gain from your challenges until the advantages outnumber the disadvantages by at least 3 to 1. Get to 5 to 1 if you can.

Step 5

Act. In unison: On your mark, get set, go! Mobilize yourself and others. Maximize the opportunities. Minimize the losses.

BEAT THE ODDS ...
CHANGE THE GAME

Bigger Challenge = Bigger Impact

Beating the odds means succeeding despite the fact that the probability of winning is low. When this happens, you change the rules of the game.

Being powerful and influential enough to "change the game" in any arena of life is intoxicating and exciting. Especially if your aims connect to wider-world benefits. It just doesn't get any better than that:

- Your confidence and courage grow
- Your gratitude expands
- Your know-how moves to the next level

JOIN FORCES

Role Models

- **Lance Armstrong** beat the odds by triumphing over cancer and used that as his driving force to change the sport of cycling forever. "Live Strong" is a mantra and a movement. Seven consecutive Tour de France yellow jerseys form an amazing record that provides others with hope and inspiration.

- **Starbucks** beat the odds that people would actually pay $3.00 for a cup of coffee and changed the game in the coffee business. A neighborhood gathering place with a premium coffee experience is now the standard for the industry. "Iced caramel sugar free skim macchiato, anyone?"

- In 2005, Australian physicians **Robin Warren** and **Barry Marshal** were awarded the Nobel Prize in medicine for discovering that stomach ulcers are caused by a strain of bacteria. Warren and Marshall fought for years to override the prevailing theory that ulcers were caused by excess stomach acids. Thanks to their game-changing beliefs, antibiotics have replaced unnecessary surgery in the treatment of ulcers.

What can you do to beat the odds and change the game in your worlds? Learn how one motivated woman in Seattle did just that.

ABT Impact Story
Meru Meets Microsoft

Iris Lemmer

One hundred women entrepreneurs in Meru, Kenya beat the odds by creating and operating sustainable, profitable online businesses. Thanks to matchmaker Iris Lemmer, these Meru entrepreneurs are learning to:

• Use Microsoft technology, tools, and resources
• Connect to financial support through microloans
• Source, market, and sell their goods over the Internet
• Establish the infrastructure necessary to grow their business

Iris's "day job" is talent management consultant at Microsoft Corporation. Her "night job" is to make a bigger impact in the wider world by bringing Microsoft technology to women in Third World countries. She picked Kenya as her place to start because of its local "assets." Kenya has one of the highest literacy rates in Africa, and the people in the community, local schools, and leaders are committed to learning and improving standards of living. The potential positive impact and ripple effect of Iris's project are awesome:

• Better educated children
• Improved family health care
• Higher household income
• Longer life expectancy (current average is 48 years)

Iris applied ABT to attract others to join forces with her in pursuit of her mighty cause. Her band of positive co-conspirators is impressive:

• Kay Felkins, from Loyola University in Chicago
• Innovative, grassroots change agents within Microsoft
• The NGO, Africa Circle of Hope
• Microsoft IdeAgency
• Local Kenyans who run the Computer Technology Center

Beyond the obvious "on the ground" benefits in Kenya and the personal gratification for Iris and her colleagues, Microsoft gains valuable insights into the use of technology in the developing world. Still in its infancy, the project can lead to further innovation through the creative use of technology and inspire new mighty cause advocates within Microsoft.

TRADE ENRAGED FOR ENGAGED

The devastation of 9/11 will long be remembered. What also lives on in our memories are the remarkable acts of leadership and recovery in the aftermath. Mayor Rudy Giuliani provided us with a prime example of Asset-Based Thinking. He made heroism more important than terrorism. He biased his attention (and the attention of the entire world) in favor of the heroic acts of courage and compassion displayed by firefighters, police, civil servants, and the general public.

Like Giuliani, people everywhere found ways to let their feelings of hope, compassion, and gratitude override their more negative emotions.

BE EMOTIONAL

By paying more attention to what inspires you and heartens you, you make better decisions and have a bigger positive impact than when you are at the mercy of anxiety or rage.

Let Emotion Reign

Emotions govern our thoughts, decisions, and actions more than we imagine. New findings in the field of neuroscience refute the conventional wisdom that emotions are subservient to rational thought. We've all heard the admonition, "Don't let your decisions be clouded by your emotions." In practical terms this just isn't possible. Emotions do influence our thoughts. Here's how the process works.

Negative Emotions	Positive Emotions
▼	▼
SET OFF ALARMS	RELEASE INCENTIVE INDICATORS
▼	▼
TRIGGER DEFICIT-BASED THINKING	TRIGGER ASSET-BASED THINKING

During 9/11, both sides of the emotional spectrum were at work. Fears and anger provoked DBT scrutiny about what went wrong. Simultaneously, the emotions of compassion, hope, and pride promoted recognition of what went right. We celebrated those who rose to the occasion, and recognized and praised the good in people.

Both emotion channels provide important inputs. When you emphasize positive ABT emotions over negative DBT emotions, your impact comes faster and goes deeper.

When we die and go to meet our Maker, we are not going to be asked why we didn't become a Messiah or find a cure for cancer. Instead, we will be asked, "Why didn't you become you?"

ELIE WIESEL

Remember … emotions reign. Be aware of how you feel. Stack the deck in favor of positive emotions with Asset-Based Thinking, no matter how challenging the circumstances.

With **Negative** Emotions – Cooperate, Don't Control

When something happens to stop progress or block your impact, it's natural to become anxious or angry. Relate to your disturbing emotions as you would to a disturbing person. Step outside the heat of the emotion. Be curious about what triggered the feelings. Go with the emtional flow until you feel calmer, less agitated. Empathize with your feelings until your fear or anger lessens. Let the intensity of anger and anxiety melt into sadness or hurt. These less intense negative emotions will help you make better, wiser decisions about how to move forward.

With **Positive** Emotions – Engage and Expand

Whenever you feel exuberance, thrill, excitement, or joy, savor and extend the experience. Express what you are feeling out loud to yourself and to others. Notice and celebrate the by-products of your positive emotions... energy, enthusiasm, creative momentum. See how others attach to your elevated mood. Let these feelings dominate your thoughts, decisions, and actions. Let them squeeze out disturbing emotions.

When you invite positive emotions to lead the way you maximize your impact in all matters.

LIVE LEGACIES NOW

In his commencement address at Stanford University, Steve Jobs (founder of Apple) revealed that he looks in the mirror every morning and asks himself:

"If I die tonight, will I be glad that I did what I am planning to do today? If the answer is 'No,' I change the plan."

This question keeps him on track, clear, and on purpose. It's not a morbid filter: just the opposite. It is a filter that enriches and inspires him to live his legacy now – before it's too late.

Leaving a legacy makes your life meaningful. Living your legacy changes the game. Imagine how invigorating and reassuring it would be to know that what you are doing right now is contributing to your legacy. Imagine how inspired others would be if they saw you building your legacy in the present.

TRY THIS:

Make Mortality Your Ally

PLANT SEEDS

Let Steve Jobs be a role model for 21 days
(the time it takes to form a habit). Ask yourself his question or one that suits you even
better. View mortality as a teacher or coach
who can guide your everyday actions. Notice
the shifts in your priorities. Notice which ac-
tivities are important as you raise the stakes
on how best to live this day of life.

No legacy is so rich as honesty.

WILLIAM SHAKESPEARE

131

ABT Impact Story
From debilitation to determination:

Sometimes a legacy is handed to you by chance or circumstance. Fate can be a boon or a burden. Lynn Fielder has Parkinson's disease. Her moving essay describes her determination and resolve to view her illness as fuel for living her legacy now.

PERSEVERE

Ten Minutes in a Body with Parkinson's: A Legacy Worth Living

The clock ticks.

I open my eyes and another day begins in which I am the intimate witness of the struggle between my brain and my body – the brain and body of a 45-year-old wife and mother with Parkinson's Disease.

The alarm rings. I wake up.

My body is stuck to the bed, stiff and uncomfortable; I have not moved a muscle during the night. I want to lounge a few minutes and ask my husband, "How was my night? Did I keep you awake with vivid, vocal dreams; I don't remember." But I abandon such congenial chitchat because my body is giving me two contradictory messages: "Get to the bathroom right away," and "I'm not moving."

My brain is running on empty in regards to dopamine levels. (With the onset of Parkinson's it is estimated that 80% of dopamine-producing brain cells are lost.) I was diagnosed 14 years ago with a newborn baby in my arms and my career ascending. Now four years into post–forced retirement, I am giving new meaning to the term "stay-at-home mom." When my daughter needs to be picked up from school I often have to tell her I won't be coming until

my body unfreezes and I overcome my temporary paralysis.

The clock ticks. I'm still not moving.

Every 3 hours, I depend upon a handful of life-giving pills to regain my mobility. They eventually lose their effectiveness, and without dopamine the brain can't tell the body to move. Physically it feels like moving-through-a-vat-of-very-thick-molasses-paralysis, or being Velcro'd-to-every-surface-paralysis. It's like a union strike: "Labor isn't budging despite what management says!"

With the help of grab bars on the bed and my strategically placed wheelchair, I am finally up!

This is how Parkinson's disease shapes my everyday life and challenges me as a wife, a mother, a daughter. Parkinson's defies me to get out of bed in the morning, dares me to keep on living. But it also shapes my legacy. Parkinson's moves and motivates me to be a tireless and vital advocate for stem cell research. Every morning I wake up with more commitment, more resolve. Every day I say "Yes, I'm here, life is good." This day makes a difference, and so will I.

Lynn Fielder

JOHN GARDNER

There's something I know about you that you may or may not know about yourself. You have within you more resources of energy than have even been tapped, more talent than has ever been exploited, more strength than has ever been tested, more to give than you have ever given.

> *…Every human being is not one but two. One is the person who we have become through the journey of the past. The other one is the dormant being of the future who we could become through our forward journey.*
>
> C. OTTO SCHARMER

CHANGE THE WAY YOU SEE THE FUTURE

ONWARD

CONVENTIONAL WISDOM

- The future is tomorrow
- The future is uncertain and daunting
- The future can be planned
- The future can be predicted

CONVENTIONAL VIEWS OF THE FUTURE: LINEAR, ANALYTICAL, PREDICTABLE

Wondering, planning, and dreaming are uniquely human capacities. We divide time into three categories: past, present, and future. These conventional categories structure the type of thinking we do relative to each time zone. We remember the past. We attend to the present. We envision the future. These parameters are useful, but limit our ability to shape the future.

IN PART FOUR YOU CAN RE-
HEARSE THE FUTURE BEFORE
IT HAPPENS. THIS DRESS RE-
HEARSAL IS YOUR MOST VALUABLE
ASSET IN ENSURING THAT YOU
WILL BE PREPARED FOR WHATEVER
HAPPENS. CHANGE THE WAY YOU
SEE YOUR FUTURE ... SO YOU CAN
CREATE IT AND LIVE IT!

ABT INSIGHTS

- The future is today
- The future is expansive and inviting
- The future can be rehearsed
- The future can be created

ABT PERSPECTIVES ON THE FUTURE: EMERGENT, INTUITIVE, TRANSFORMATIONAL

Asset-Based Thinking collapses the boundaries between past, present, and future, allowing you to focus on all of them simultaneously. You learn to create and tell detailed stories about the future you most desire, as if it had already happened. You make a memory and a vision all at once. The narrative power of ABT stories creates worthwhile visions of the future that come to life in the present. You become the author and producer of the future you most want so you can live it right now.

BOLD BEGINNINGS.
GREAT ENDINGS.

Everyone loves a good story. Colloquialisms such as "You have a flair for the dramatic" and "What's your story?" reflect our tendency to see life through a narrative lens. People from all walks of life have the capacity to understand the lives they lead as a coherent story. It comes to us naturally.

Bring Your Future to Life

To make the most of your future see yourself as an adventurer.

Picture yourself as the primary author and driving force of your story. Seize your inner power to direct and shape it, deriving energy from your circles of influence and the ripple effects of your signature impact.

Who controls the past controls the future: who controls the present controls the past.

GEORGE ORWELL

THE FUTURE
FRAMES
THE PRESENT

Imagining the detail of your future as a current reality requires going beyond the constraints and assumptions of "the way things are now" or simple "what if" fantasies. Imagining your best future and how to realize it requires you to think out of the box and deep inside yourself simultaneously.

You have to clearly see and feel your future.

The details of your future can be hard to picture. To make them accessible and invigorating, follow the techniques of the great storytellers and moviemakers. The ABT tools that follow provide the direction and storyboard templates for you to create and star in your personal adventure story. Have fun!

> *I look to the future because that's where I'm going to spend the rest of my life.*
>
> GEORGE BURNS (SAID AT AGE 87)

A SNEAK PREVIEW OF
YOUR BEST FUTURE

Giving yourself a sneak preview of the full-length version of your vision helps you see the arc of the whole story. Enjoy yourself. Do these five things:

Activate Your Motivation:

State your beliefs and passions. Articulate your mighty cause. Ignite your imagination and get your creative juices flowing by reminding yourself why you want to make this particular future happen.

See the Big Picture:

Imagine the future you most desire as if it has already happened. Make it reality. See the full context of each situation. Visualize what has happened to you and to those you will influence and touch. Feel your impact.

Frame the Plot Line:

Let the story unfold in your mind's eye. Be adventuresome. Playful. Imagine vividly and in great detail the key episodes of your future as they unfold ... victories, defeats, highs and lows ... get a glimpse of them all.

Assemble Your Cast and Crew:

Visualize the important people who are part of your story – mentors, allies, naysayers, detractors, sponsors. Cast them in their roles. Rehearse various encounters. Say "Thank you" to everyone.

See the Stories One by One:

Let the stories form like movie trailers in your mind.

Always remember that imagining your future is a creative, generative act that shapes what happens.

Imagine your future often.

STORYBOARD YOUR ADVENTURE

All you need is your imagination, a pencil, and a piece of paper.

Before the filmmaker says, "Lights, camera, action," the director has a script. The scenes and sequences of the film are blocked out. This is the storyboard that depicts how the visual components and the narrative layout of the film work together. It directs the creative process for the set designer, the cinematographer, the actors, and the editor.

Storyboarding is a creative process that both inspires and directs. In a simplified form, it will help you craft the vision of what you want to make happen from start to finish.

You will create the story of your future in three parts:

Part 1: Unleash Your Power
Part 2: Expand Your Influence
Part 3: Maximize Your Impact

These three parts correspond to the three phases of every great mythical adventure. Joseph Campbell, scholar and teacher, discovered predictable storytelling stages across all cultures. From *Beowulf* to *Star Wars*, heroes say yes to The Call, set forth on The Adventure, and Return Home with amazing prizes.

Let the storyboard instructions guide you and help you get ready to write the story of your heroic adventure.

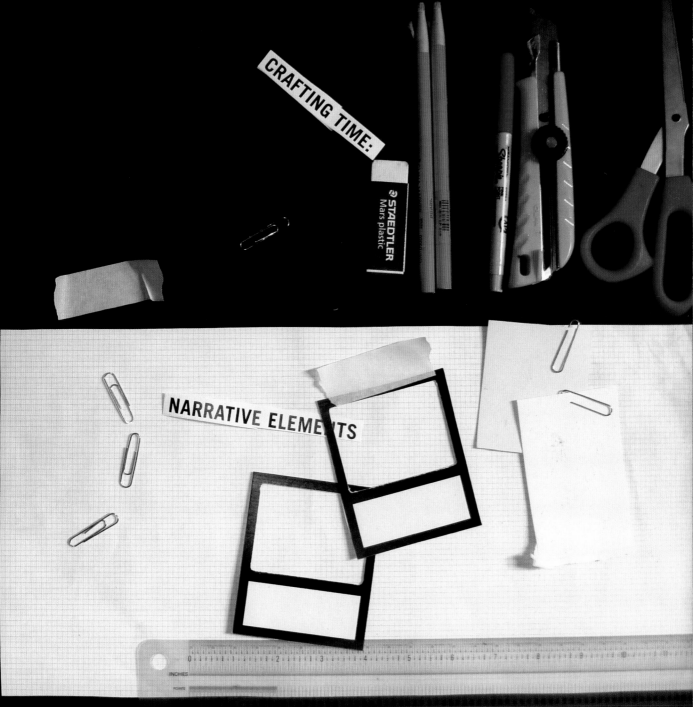

SET THE SCENE: PART 1

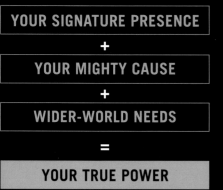

YOUR SIGNATURE PRESENCE

+

YOUR MIGHTY CAUSE

+

WIDER-WORLD NEEDS

=

YOUR TRUE POWER

Nature arms each man with some faculty which enables him to do easily some feat impossible to any other.

Unleash Your Power!

This ABT equation is the foundation of true power. As in most adventures, you, the central character, will experience longings and urges to move beyond the ho-hum of everyday life. At this junction you are restless and uneasy and crave more meaning and purpose. Realizing your purpose and serving your mighty cause feed your spirit of adventure.

Then, as with any adventure, you will experience a struggle between two opposing forces … the "drag" of practicality and resignation and the "pull" of possibility and hope.

These forces take the form of both encouraging and discouraging voices from inside your own mind and out of the mouths of others. You must listen to and learn from all of them but the voices of possibility and hope win out. Hear yourself say "yes" to your call to adventure.

NARRATIVE ELEMENTS:

Name the types of causes, possibilities and dreams that are calling you. Select your most compelling agenda. The one that will capture your mind, heart, and spirit and ignite your devotion.

Take a fresh look at your notes and impressions from Part 1. These are the "how to" footage from which you craft Part I of your adventure storyboard.

- Great Beginnings
- Your Signature Presence
- Your Personal Platform
- ABT Life Map

Notice How:

1. Your previous reflections provide insight into your deepest purpose and most motivating causes
2. Your passions intersect with your talents
3. You mesh what you want with what the world wants most from you.

Listen between the lines.

Pay attention to any internal voices that encourage or discourage you. Take note of the arguments "for" and "against" embarking on this adventure. Let both sides of the ledger inform and inspire.

Give credence to the "pros" and "cons" but give more weight to the "pros."

As you lean in the direction of saying "yes," let your attraction to your cause pull you forward. This positive pull creates your momentum. If all you are doing is pushing yourself forward, you will run out of energy too soon.

Your ability to see your adventure through to the end and return home in victory is sustained by saying "yes."

My Signature Presence

YOUR MIGHTY CAUSE

CRAFTING TIME:

**My manifesto
I believe in**

**My Signature
Presence**

Collect Your Assets:

Use the storyboard template to capture the source of your personal power and the essence of your call to adventure. First, write and visualize this part of your adventure story, then tell it out loud to one person you trust. Feel yourself tell the story. Then retell it again to yourself and others. Try this even if you feel hesitant. Each time you tell the story, envision it coming true. See it as it shapes your new reality.

Step 1:

Describe the nature of your internal imperatives and your mighty cause. Give reasons why you think this pursuit is so valuable and important. Say what it will do, who will benefit, how things will be different.

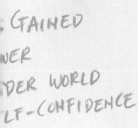

GAINED
WER
DER WORLD
LF-CONFIDENCE

Yesterday.
Today.
Tomorrow.
Dream.

+/- = Yes!
Join Me!

Step 2:

Tell why you are so well suited to lead this charge. Name your assets, describe your Signature Presence.

Step 3:

Describe the difference between the future you seek and the current reality. How will your desired future trump the present? What will be possible then that is impossible now? Tell the story. Make promises. Commit yourself.

Step 4:

Note the pros and cons of embarking on your adventure. Describe your self-doubt. Who else is wary? List 5 persuasive arguments in favor of pursuing your aim. Ask those you trust why they support you.

SET THE SCENE PART 2

ALLIES + VICTORIES + WINDFALLS

–

ENEMIES + SETBACKS

=

INFLUENCE^2

Expand Your Circle of Influence

This ABT equation is the formula for shaping and influencing what happens around you and because of you. In the spirit of great epic stories, you encounter an evolving array of different forces – positive enabling forces that will accelerate your progress and propel you forward.

You will meet allies who will be drawn to you and some will show up unannounced. You will experience victories large and small. Surprising windfalls and blessings will come your way. You will improvise and capitalize on all of them.

And of course, the negative forces will also appear. Some mistakes, failures, setbacks will sting and "stall" you, but not defeat you. You will extract the lessons they provide and use them to master challenges and wrestle enemies to the ground. This is the side of your adventure that solidifies your commitment and sparks your resolve.

Transformation to me means the powerful unleashing of human potential to commit to, care about and change for a better life. Transformation occurs when people give up their automatic way of being and commit themselves to a different future.

NARRATIVE ELEMENTS:

Make a starter list of potential allies and enemies, door openers and roadblocks. Review some of the reflection exercises from Part 2 in which you practiced how to know someone.

- 7 Ways for 7 Days
- Trade Places
- Tell the Best Truth First
- Have Courageous Conversations
- ABT Images of Success

Develop brief scenarios of how you engaged people you met along way. How did you see the positive motives of those who tried to hold you back? How did you enroll and inspire others and appreciate their contributions? What did you say and do to celebrate them?

Be inspired by the stories of Bill Strickland, Nilaja Sun, and others you admire. Let their attractive qualities seep into the essence of who you are. Imagine the moments you turned feelings of threats into the positive energy of a challenge. How did you move from anxiety to anticipation? What personal assets did you rely on to overcome the obstacles and setbacks along the way?

My Influence Quotient

!!!

Courageous Conversations
"Trading Places"

CRAFTING TIME:

Assemble Your Circles of Influence

Recognize the "ups" of those who supported you and the "downs" of those who got in your way. Write this portion of your adventure as if you have already experienced it. Give yourself permission to embellish or even exaggerate what happened for the sake of making it vividly real.

Make "Eye"-to-"I" Contact / See deeper

Step 1:
Describe the family members, colleagues, friends, and neighbors who have become your staunchest supporters. Whose support surprised you? Describe the interactions that meant the most to you.

Step 2:
Describe the nay-sayers and obstructionists. Select only a few. That's all you need.

Step 3:
Craft scenarios that depict your victories and windfalls. Put yourself in the picture by expressing your excitement and identifying what you did to capitalize on every moment of progress.

Step 4:
Conjure up the pitfalls and setbacks that you encountered and mastered. Write specific examples of the skills and talents you drew upon to overcome them.

Step 5:
Recall and describe the pros and cons that impacted you most. Then summarize the 5 best concrete reasons why you must pursue your aim. Ask those you admire and trust why they support you.

BER:
ONTACT
RATION
UP

Listen Softer
Hear More

Give Truth the Upper Hand
Speak it

Earn a Standing
Ovation

Admire
Someone

Self: How you will grow and change for the better.

Others: How you and your cause will touch and transform everyone you encounter.

Situations: How circumstances, events, and the contexts within which you operate will evolve and improve you and your worlds.

PERSONAL PURPOSE
×
PASSION

+

COLLECTIVE MOMENTUM

=

MAXIMUM IMPACT

Ensure Maximum Impact

This ABT equation identifies the variables that yield maximum impact. Your adventure would feel hollow and empty if your efforts never paid off. With ABT you realize that the "payoff" is also in your progress. Every major step taken, each milestone of progress creates impact that builds exponentially. At the end of the road, you will be able to see and signify the full depth and breadth of your impact by illuminating in three directions.

In this final scene, you chronicle lessons learned, leaps forward in skill and confidence, frontiers crossed and the accumulation of authentic credibility. You will return home profoundly changed for the better with a boon of prizes you never imagined. Conjure up the benefits you want for yourself and others. Let yourself be surprised in advance, invigorated by those you will touch and how they join you.

Tell how your cause has "fired you up" and how it will catch fire beyond you. See the ABT ripple effect really come into play. Make it count by stretching your mind, spirit, and heart beyond their comfort zone. See the positive impacts that abound.

NARRATIVE ELEMENTS:

Part 3 is the culmination of your adventure that depicts how things come together for the greater good. Write your impact message in one sentence. Distill the meaning of your quest into a concentrated dose of inspiration. This is the essence from which all else will flow. Your sentence might sound like a mantra or movie subtitle. You might fashion it as a headline, proverb, or famous quote. Some ABT inspirational one-liners that come to mind:

Yoda :
"There is no try"
Louis Brandeis:
"Sunlight is the best disinfectant"
Peter Pan:
"First star to the right and straight on 'til morning"
Buzz Lightyear:
"To infinity and beyond"

Create your own by building on the inspiration and vision of others. Dive into the spirit of your adventure. Let its main meaning shine through your words. It's your adventure to name.

Next, glance over the chapter titles in the table of contents to stimulate the types of impact stories you will select. See what lessons, prizes, advances, and achievements they trigger as you describe the many impacts of your adventure.

Review your ABT impact exercises, too:
Start Small, Win Fast
Make Opposition Your Ally
With Negative Emotions –
   Cooperate Don't Control
With Positive Emotions –
   Engage and Expand
Make Mortality Your Ally

My Signature
Impact

Live My Legacy
NOW

CRAFTING TIME:

See Your Signature Impacts

Create the crescendo of your future come true. This part of your story packs the punch and the propellant that make embarking on the adventure worthwhile. Write it with gusto. Let your flair for the dramatic show up. Subtle is sometimes just as dramatic as bold. Make the end of the story fit your personal style. Let your Signature Presence shine through. You will probably find that telling yourself and others how the story ends is most compelling of all. Have fun!

Change the
Game Impact

Step 1:

Impacts on You Before and After
Who you were before the adventure, compared to afterward.
What shifted? Claim all the ground you've gained in values, aspirations, insights, attitudes, and skills.
Write with the exuberance and pride of a job well done.

Step 2:

Impacts on Others
Write the credits: who are your costars in the adventure? Identify their assets and contributions.
What you admire and appreciate most about their roles.
How did this adventure change each costar for the better?

Step 3:

Impacts on Situations
Narrate the transformation: describe how all aspects of your life evolved and improved as if it were a panoramic photo.
Let the impact stories radiate out.

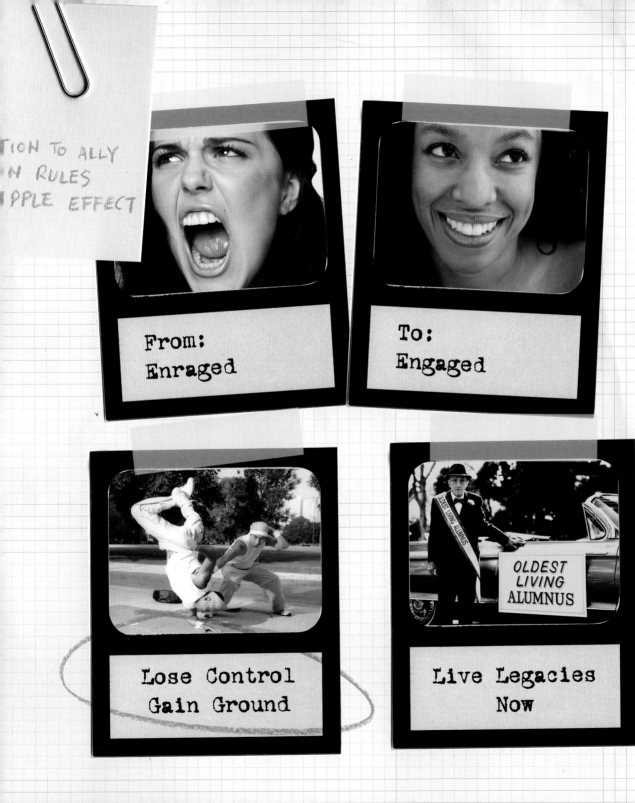

TION TO ALLY
N RULES
PPLE EFFECT

From:
Enraged

To:
Engaged

Lose Control
Gain Ground

OLDEST LIVING ALUMNUS

Live Legacies
Now

165

SEE YOUR FUTURE COME TRUE

Now it's time for you to assemble the elements of your story, put the parts together, and see your great adventure unfold. Step back and see the flow of your story, the details and nuances. Here's where you get to edit, tweak, and add the finishing touches and get it ready for its premiere.

You see it, feel it all, and are inspired. Then comes the best part. You're ready to watch the elements of your future come to life right before your eyes. Show and tell the world the good news about the future as it comes true. Remember, this is your mighty cause brought to life in the power of your Signature Presence, ready to expand your Circles of Influence and unleash your Signature Impact.

Your Adventure Story. Enjoy and celebrate its premiere.

POWER

INFLUENCE

IMPACT

Someplace along the line the audience discovers you. In my case it was playing the Gipper.

RONALD REAGAN

KATHRYN D. CRAMER

Kathryn D. Cramer, Ph.D., is a licensed psychologist and founder of The Cramer Institute in St. Louis. She and her colleagues at The Cramer Institute have pioneered Asset-Based Thinking approaches to coaching, consulting, and training for more than twenty years. Under Kathy's leadership, organizations such as Monsanto, DuPont, Microsoft, Starbucks, Peabody Energy, Deloitte & Touche, Master-Card, and the US Air Force have adopted ABT approaches to developing their leaders and managing change.

Kathy is an accomplished author and keynote speaker as well as an experienced consultant and executive coach. She is the author of four previous books including the most recent, **Change the Way You See Everything Through Asset-Based Thinking** (Running Press, 2006).

Dr. Cramer earned a Master's degree in psychology from DePauw University and a doctorate in psychology from St. Louis University. She founded the Stress Center at St. Louis University Medical Center and served as its director for nine years. Dr. Cramer is a member of the American Psychological Association. She currently serves on the board for the St. Louis Psychoanalytic Institute and the executive advisory board for the John Cook School of Business at St. Louis University.

HANK WASIAK

Hank Wasiak is a communications industry leader who has worked with the corporate elite of global business. He is cofounder of The Concept Farm, one of today's hottest creative development companies. Hank is an Emmy award–winning producer and TV host, author, entrepreneur, and teacher.

Hank has risen to the top of every organization he was with and retired as vice chairman of McCann Erickson WorldGroup, the world's largest marketing communications company, to cofound The Concept Farm.

Hank is executive producer and segment host of the company's Emmy award–winning weekly series *Cool In Your Code*, and he's won two Emmy awards for his innovative interview series, *Back on The Block*. Hank teamed up with Kathy Cramer to create the first book in this series, *Change the Way You See Everything*.

Hank earned a Bachelors degree in Advertising from Pace University and an MBA in marketing from the Baruch School of Business, has held an assistant professorship at Pace University, and has taught at Eckerd College, the University of South Florida, and the University of Louisville. Hank serves on the board of the Founders Affilliate of the American Heart Association. He is also a Reiki Master.

THINKERS WHO INSPIRE

Juanita Brown
Founder of the World Café and has spread this ABT process worldwide to help individuals engage in meaningful and important dialogue about issues and questions that matter.

Marcus Buckingham
Former senior researcher for the Gallup Organization. Author of best-selling books: *First, Break All the Rules* (coauthored with Curt Coffman); *Now, Discover Your Strengths* (coauthored with Donald O. Clifton); and *The One Thing You Need to Know*, in which the author gives important insights to maximizing strengths, understanding the crucial differences between leadership and management, and fulfilling the quest for long-lasting personal success.

David Cooperrider
Founder and practitioner of the concept Appreciative Inquiry; has developed a methodology that assists organizations in shaping their future from the positive core of what already exists and what is already working.

Rob Cross
Author of T*he Hidden Power of Social Networks: Understanding How Work Really Gets Done in Organizations*. Professor of management at the University of Virginia and research director of The Network Roundtable, a consortium of 55 organizations sponsoring research on network applications to critical management issues.

Mihaly Csikszentmihalyi
Professor at University of Chicago, the author of several books including *Flow: The Psychology of Optimal Experience*. He identifies the state of being engaged so fully in what we are doing, with just the right amount of stretch, that we are deeply satisfied and literally lose track of time.

Alan Deutschman
One of America's leading writers on change and innovation. Author of groundbreaking book, *Change or Die: The Three Keys to Change at Work and in Life*, which debunks myths about this crucial topic and reveals what actually inspires and motivates real change. Executive director of Unboundary, a strategy consulting firm.

Malcolm Gladwell
Staff writer with *The New Yorker* since 1996. In 2005 he was named one of *Time Magazine's* 100 Most Influential People. Author of two books, *The Tipping Point: How Little Things Make a Big Difference* (2000); and *Blink: The Power of Thinking Without Thinking* (2005).

Daniel P. Goleman
Psychologist, former reporter for the *New York Times*. His 1995 book *Emotional Intelligence* was a breakthrough in the study of EQ. Argues in this and subsequent books, including the recent *Social Intelligence*, that emotional intelligence is as or more important to work success than technical skills or practical knowledge

Dr. John Gottman
Cofounder of the Gottman Institute with his wife, Dr. Julie Schwartz Gottman. Executive director of the nonprofit Relationship Research Institute; Dr. Gottman is an emeritus professor of psychology at the University of Washington and founded what the media termed "The Love Lab."

Chip Heath and Dan Heath
Brothers and coauthors of the book *Made to Stick: Why Some Ideas Survive and Others Die*, which has been a *New York Times*, *Wall Street Journal*, and *Business Week* best seller. Write a monthly column called "Made To Stick" for *Fast Company* magazine. Speak and consult on the topic of "making ideas stick."

Joseph Jaworski
Cofounder of the Centre for Generative Leadership, designed to help companies and other organizations develop the leadership required to shape the future. Coauthor of *Presence* and author of *Synchronicity: The Inner Path to Leadership*.

THINKERS WHO INSPIRE

Mel Levine, M.D.
Educator and author of *A Mind at a Time*, an Asset-Based thinker who has contributed significantly to our understanding of individual differences in children's learning styles, skills, and talents.

Parker Palmer
Author, educator, and activist who focuses on issues in education, community, leadership, spirituality, and social change; founded the Center for Courage & Renewal, which oversees the "Courage to Teach" program for K–12 educators across the country and parallel programs for people in other professions, including medicine, law, ministry, and philanthropy.

Sara Orem, Ph.D.
Adjunct professor of management in the graduate business program at Capella University and principal of Lotus Coaching. Has presented programs in Appreciative Inquiry at OD Network and the Transformative Learning Conference. Coauthor of *Appreciative Coaching*.

Harrison Owen
Founder and creator of Open Space, offers this ABT methodology to organizations who want to present at meetings and conferences. It invites everyone present to teach and learn from each other.

R. Keith Sawyer
One of the country's leading experts on the science of creativity. Studies creativity, everyday conversation, children's play and everyday social life, group dynamics, and collaboration. The empowering message of his most recent book, *Group Genius,* is that all of us have the potential to be more creative; we just need to learn the secrets of group genius.

C. Otto Scharmer
Cofounder of the Leadership Lab for Social Responsibility in Business at the MIT Sloan School of Management, where he also lectures. Coauthor of *Presence: Human Purpose and the Field of the Future*, and most recently, the author of *Theory U.*

Dov Seidman
Founder and CEO of LRN. Author of *HOW: Why How We Do Anything Means Everything … in Business (and in Life)*, which posits that success no longer lies in what we do; how we do what we do now matters most.

Martin Seligman
Professor of psychology at University of Pennsylvania and author of *Learned Optimism* and *Authentic Happiness*, scholar and thought leader in understanding optimism.

Peter Senge
Coauthor of *Presence: Human Purpose and the Field of the Future*. Pioneer of the concept, "learning organization." Studied at MIT how firms and organizations develop adaptive capabilities. 1990 book *The Fifth Discipline* brought him firmly into the limelight and popularized the concept of the "learning organization."

William Ury
Author of *Getting to Yes, Getting Past No, The Power of the Positive No*, and *Getting to Peace*. Each of these books demonstrates ways of finding the common ground among people with differences and tapping into the collective strengths and talents of those present.

Marvin Weisbord and Sandra Janoff
Creators of the Future Search process, and authors of *Future Search*, a methodology to help organizations solve critical problems through this creative and innovative process.

Joe Weller
Retired chairman and CEO of Nestlé USA; natural ABT leader in business and personal life. Remarkable track record of success at work and devotion to promoting education. Recent book, *A Blueprint for Success,* shares the principles of leadership that have informed his own success.

CREDITS

Written by
Kathryn D. Cramer, Ph.D.
Hank Wasiak

Edited by
Jennifer Kasius

Publicity
Craig Herman

Art direction + design
The Concept Farm

Creative Director
John Gellos

Art directors
Robert Singh

Designers
Sujin Kim
Hendrik Großekathöfer

Project Manager
Angel Maldonado

Photos
Getty Images (unless otherwise noted)
John Gellos (p. 16, 139)
Angel Maldonado (p. 42)
Suzy Gorman (p. 176)
Greg Lord (p. 177)

Illustrations
Hendrik Großekathöfer (p. 74)

THANKS

To the positive
coconspirators whose
Signature Presence
made this book possible ...

Sign in:

Judy Dubin

John Geller

Peggy Klout

Angel L. Maldonado Jr.

Matt Breitfelder

R. Cole

Beth Chesterton

Sherry Dodd

Michele L. Mason

Gifu Kasius

Toni Bailey

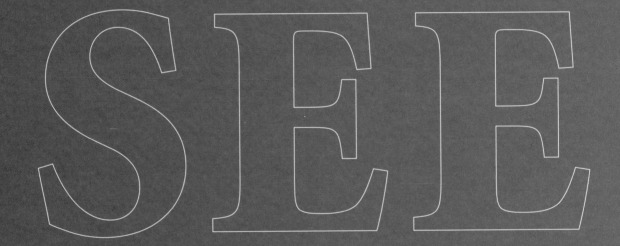